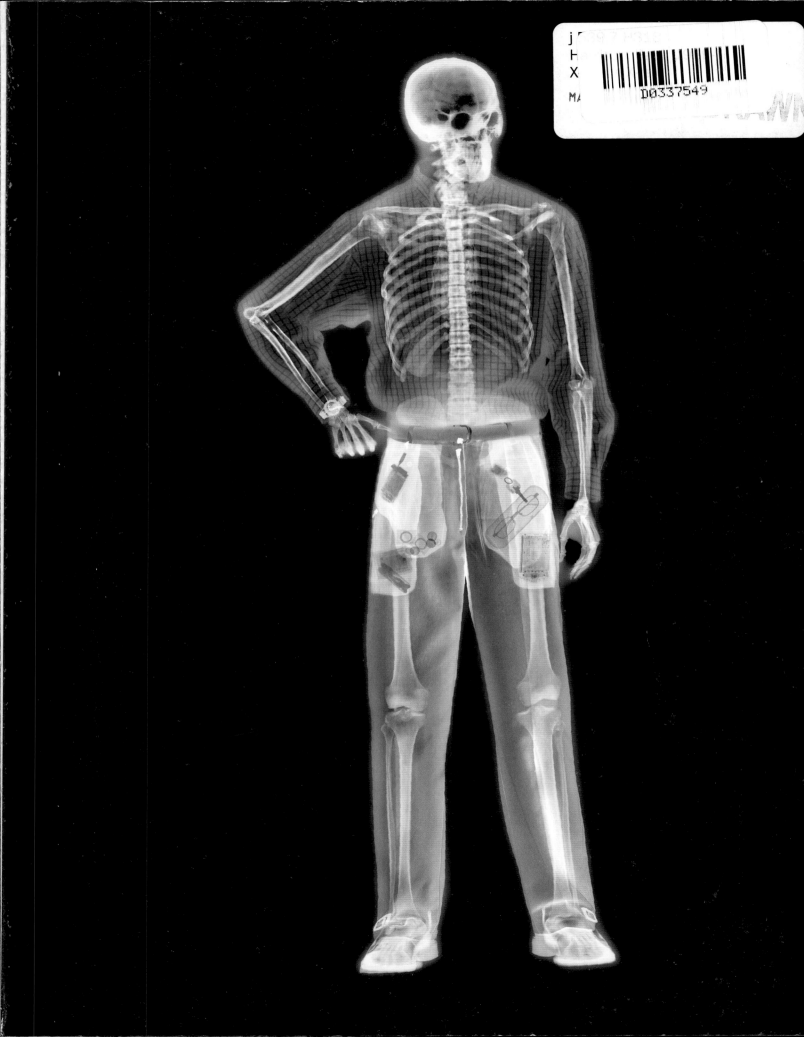

rlton Book.

hs © 2010 by Nick Veasey
esign © 2010 by Carlton Books Limited

ector: Jane Wilsher
irector: Clare Baggaley
Editor: Barry Timms
Paul Chattaway
Harrison and Barry Timms
n: Rachel Burgess
s: Selina Hurley and Rob Skitmore at
e Museum, London, and Barbara Taylor

n 2010
 Books Limited
 of the
blishing Group
er Street, London W1T 3JW

6 5 4 3 2 1

alogue record for this book is
rom the British Library.

SO D/09/6170
Heshan, China

SCHOLASTIC and associated logos are
trademarks and/or registered trademarks of
Scholastic Inc.

ISBN: 978-0-545-21847-4

Xtreme X-ray

PHOTOGRAPHS BY NICK VEASEY

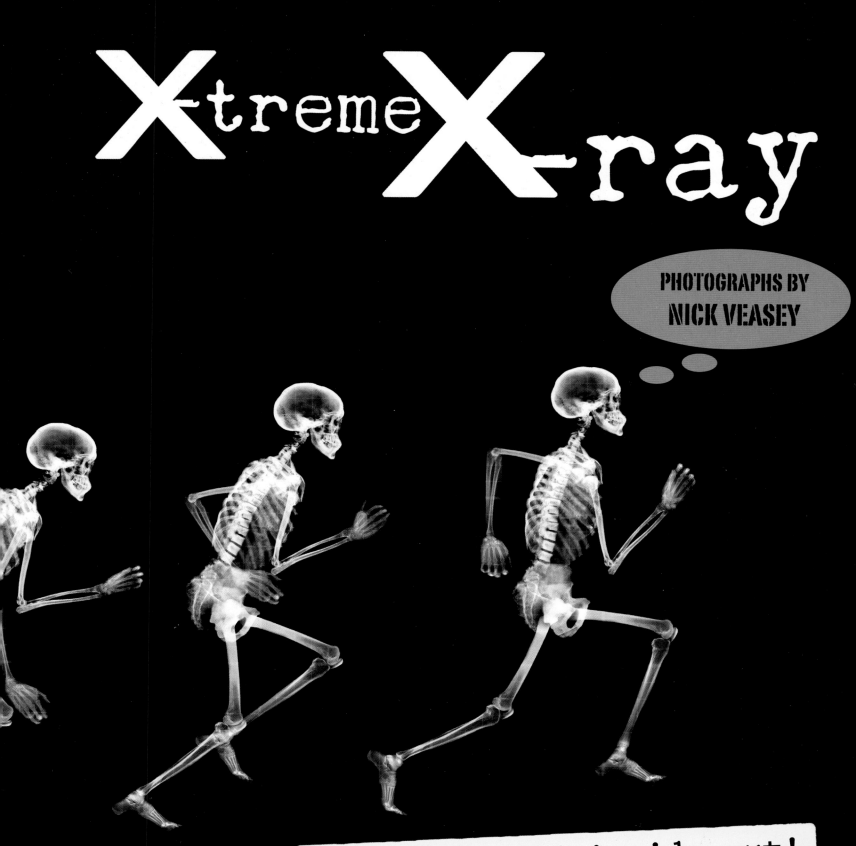

See the world inside out!

INVISIBLE RAYS

What exactly are X-rays?

X-rays are similar to the rays of light from the sun or fro
But unlike these rays of light, X-rays are normally invisib
pass right through objects instead of bouncing off the

Then how does an X-ray machine work?

The machine fires X-rays through an object and onto
surface to make a picture called a radiograph. It is p
the strength of the rays to look at different layers withi

AN AMAZING DISCOVERY

Who first discovered X-rays?

X-rays were found unexpectedly in 1895 by Wilhelm Rö
a German scientist. During a physics experiment, he no
glass tube containing electrodes was glowing. He disco
electricity passed between the electrodes, mysterious
out that showed up on a photographic plate.

Why are they called X-rays?

Wilhelm Röntgen called them X for "unknown."

WHO USES X-RAYS?

• **Doctors and dentists**
You are most likely to see X-ray equipment in hospitals and dentists' offices. Bones and teeth are the hardest parts of the body. They show up well because they absorb more X-rays than muscles or fat do.

• **Airport security guards**
X-ray machines are used at airports to check luggage. They show weapons and other unsafe objects that metal detectors might miss.

• **Archaeologists and historians**
By using fairly weak levels of radiation, archaeologists and historians can look below the surface of an old manuscript or book page to find traces of words written there previously.

• **Astronomers**
The sun, the stars, and even black holes all give off X-rays. Astronomers use these X-rays to find out more about such objects in space, which are too far away to examine in most other ways.

DANGER!

X-rays can be dangerous, and exposure to them for long periods is bad for our health. For this reason, many of the photographs in this book were put together from smaller parts, like the pieces of a jigsaw puzzle. The X-ray machine was kept in a lead-lined room to prevent the X-rays from leaking out, and the photographer stayed outside while the pictures were being taken.

HUMAN X-RAYS

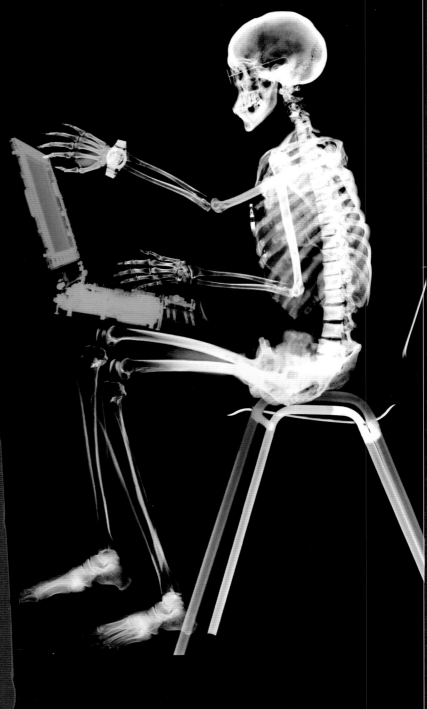

Why do we X-ray the human body?
Before the discovery of X-rays, the only way to see inside a human body was to cut one open. This had rather dangerous drawbacks if the person was still alive — such as loss of blood, infection, and even death. Being able to take X-ray photographs has changed the face of medicine. Now we can look inside and see what is wrong, with very little risk to the patient.

Are there other uses?
Yes — X-rays are not only useful for telling us about living people. They are also being used by Egyptologists, who study ancient Egypt. An X-ray machine can look straight through the bandages of a mummy and see what lies beneath, without causing any damage.

What color are X-ray photographs?
Normally, X-ray photographs are black and white. However, in this book some of the pictures have been colored to help you see the details more clearly.

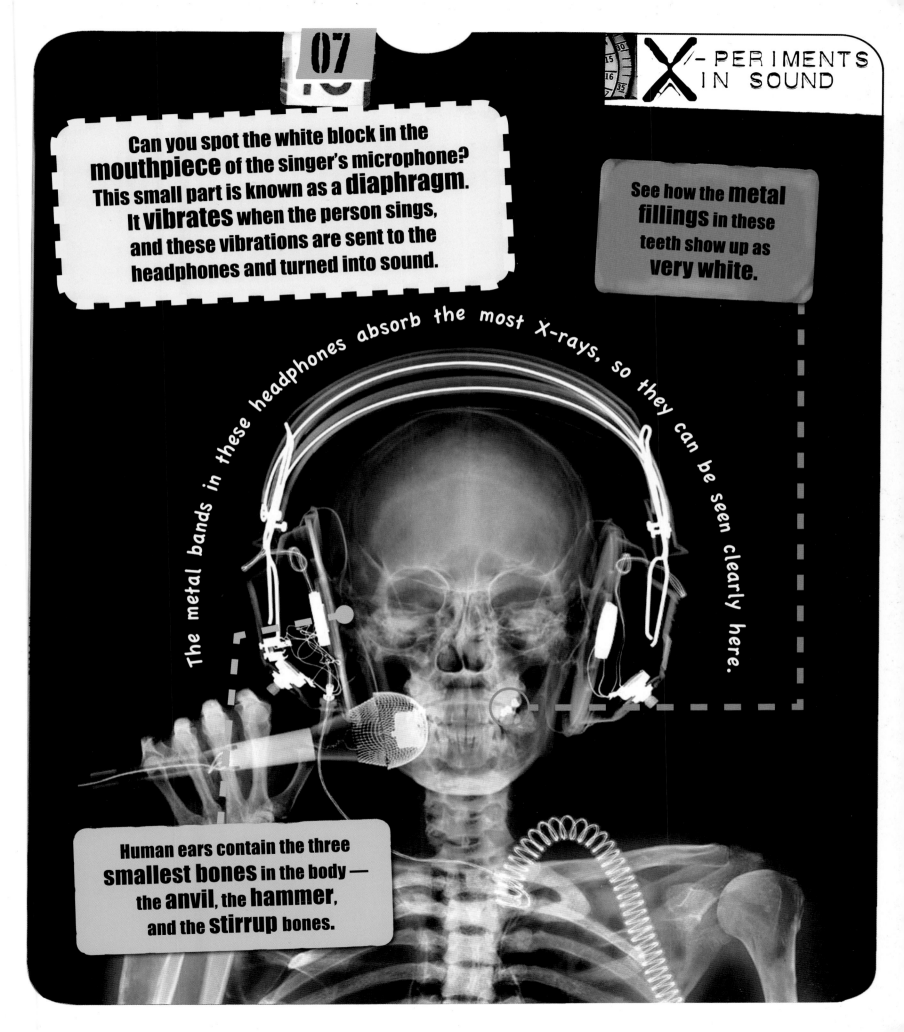

Can you spot the white block in the **mouthpiece** of the singer's microphone? This small part is known as a **diaphragm**. It **vibrates** when the person sings, and these vibrations are sent to the headphones and turned into sound.

See how the **metal fillings** in these teeth show up as **very white.**

The metal bands in these headphones absorb the most X-rays, so they can be seen clearly here.

Human ears contain the three **smallest bones** in the body — the **anvil**, the **hammer**, and the **stirrup** bones.

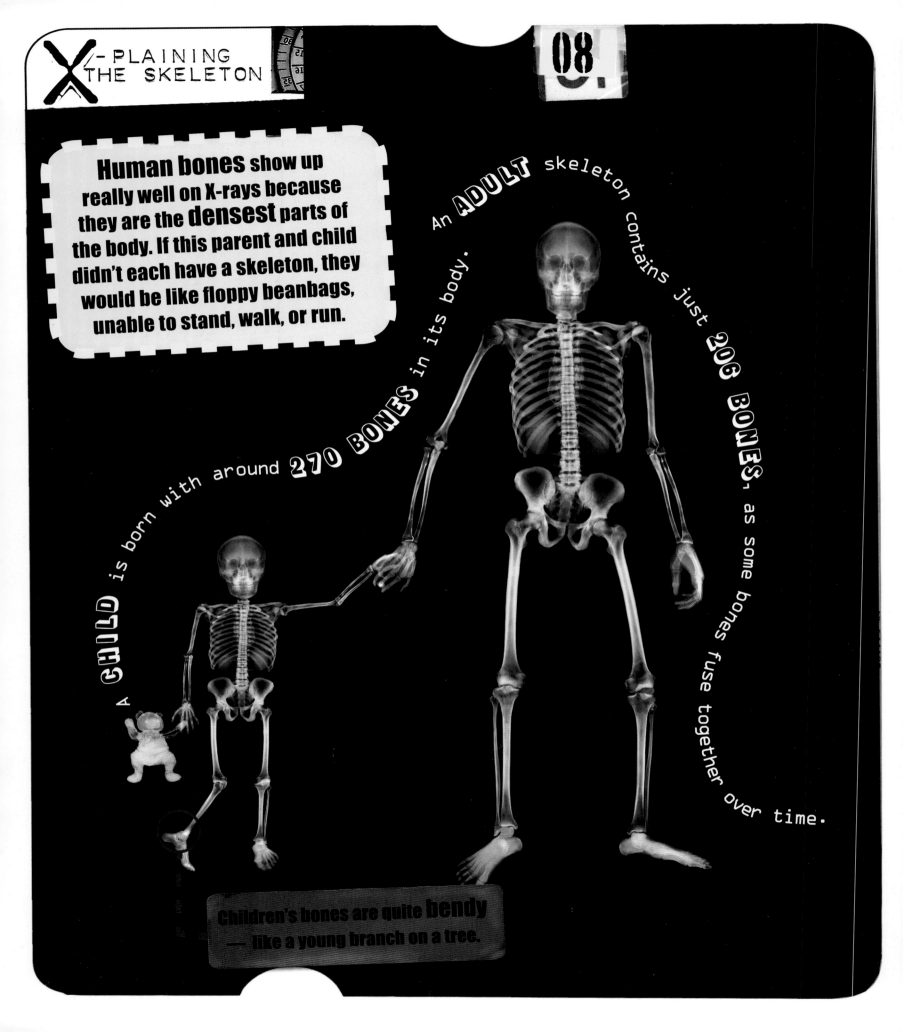

Human bones show up really well on X-rays because they are the **densest** parts of the body. If this parent and child didn't each have a skeleton, they would be like floppy beanbags, unable to stand, walk, or run.

An **ADULT** skeleton contains just **206 BONES**, as some bones fuse together over time.

A **CHILD** is born with around **270 BONES** in its body.

Children's bones are quite **bendy** — like a young branch on a tree.

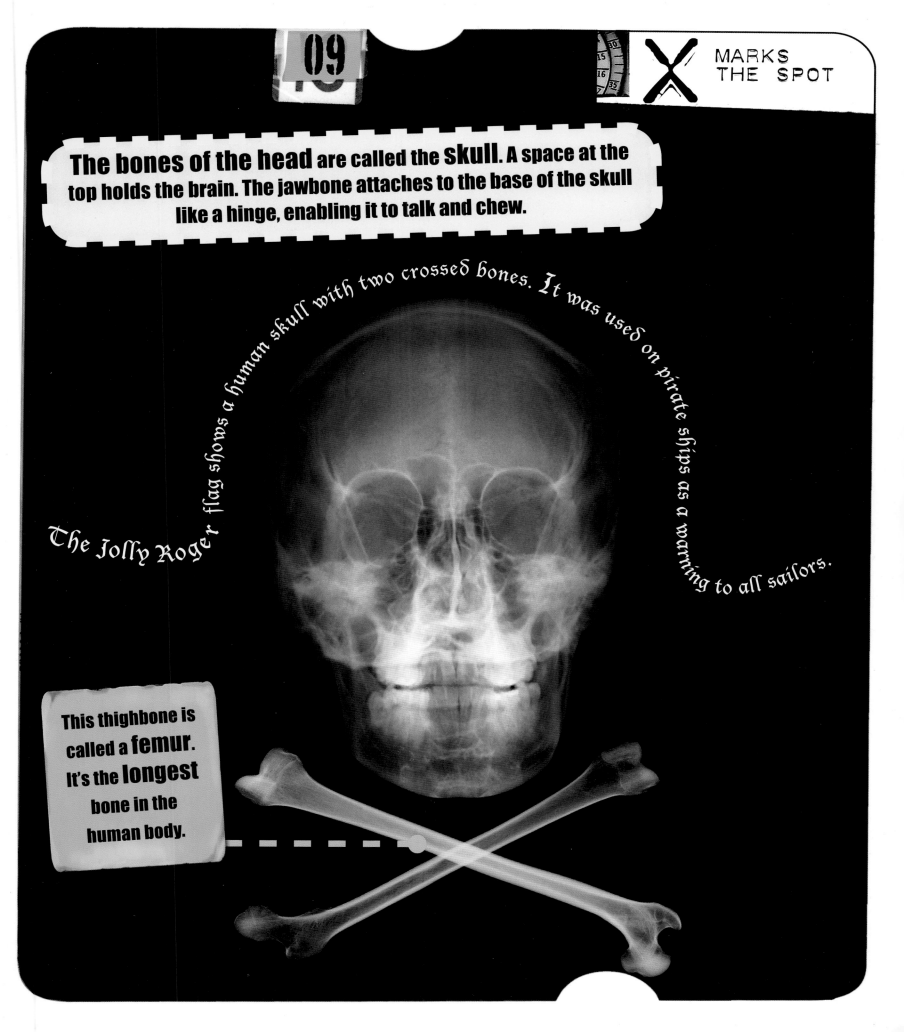

The bones of the head are called the **skull**. A space at the top holds the brain. The jawbone attaches to the base of the skull like a hinge, enabling it to talk and chew.

The Jolly Roger flag shows a human skull with two crossed bones. It was used on pirate ships as a warning to all sailors.

This thighbone is called a **femur**. It's the **longest** bone in the human body.

Imagine a **see-through bus** . . . The one shown here uses diesel fuel to take passengers from point A to point B, but back in the 1820s buses were pulled along by horses. The first public bus service was set up in 1826 in Nantes, France, by Stanislas Baudry.

The **longest bus** in the world comes from China.

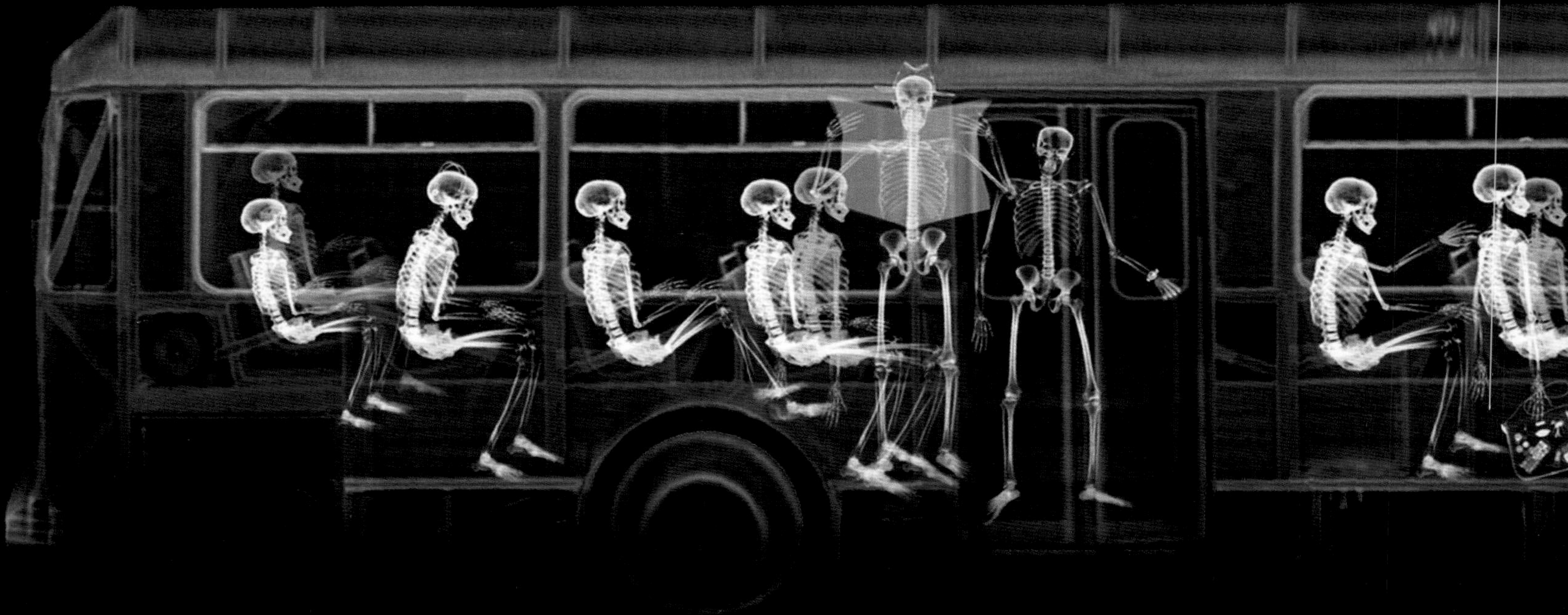

THE OLDEST ROADS HAVE BEEN FOUND IN THE

NEW YORK BUS DEPARTMENT

GROUP TICKET FOR **19** PASSENGERS — that's a grand total of **3,914** bones!

ADMIT: **19**

It has three sections and is a staggering 82 feet long!

BUS STOP

GUESS HOW MANY
BONES YOU USE
WHEN YOU RAISE
YOUR ARM TO
STOP A BUS . . .
AN AMAZING 31!

CITY OF UR, IRAQ. THEY DATE RIGHT BACK TO 4000 BC.

Why do you think these **tires** look **dark** on an X-ray? It's because they are filled with **air** rather than solid rubber.

12

Look inside this X-rayed **high-rise** building . . . What activities can you see taking place? Tall buildings are actually a very old idea. The ancient Romans called them "insulae" and were building them around 2,000 years ago.

These two men are **shaking hands** in greeting. No less than **54 bones** are at work here — 27 in each hand.

Passenger elevators were invented by **Elisha Otis** in 1852.

Bricks absorb a lot of X-rays, so they **show up** very well in X-ray photographs.

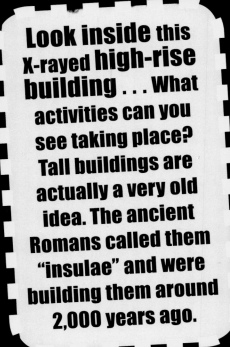

Hands up if you like X-rays! The very first X-ray photograph was of the **hand** of Anna Röntgen. She was the wife of Wilhelm Röntgen, the man who first discovered X-rays.

Most primates, including **humans,** have **opposable thumbs.** This means that the thumb can touch each finger of the hand.

X-rays do not show the **blood vessels** or **tendons** in the hand.

There are **8 bones** in a human **wrist.**

Guess which are the thickest parts of these jeans. It's the seams, which show up whiter on X-rays than the rest of the denim material. The word "denim" comes from the expression "de Nîmes," which is French for "from Nîmes," the town where the cloth was first made.

Over 14 billion zippers are made each year.

Metal coins date back to around 600 BC.

See this skeleton move!
Roller skates were first invented in 1759 by Joseph Merlin. Unfortunately, he crashed into a mirror upon giving his first demonstration. In-line skates were first patented in 1819 by a Monsieur Petitbled, but didn't become a craze until the 1990s.

Skating uses all sorts of different **muscles** in the body. They work together to maintain the skater's **balance.**

These **brakes** are made of **solid rubber,** so they show up clearly on X-rays.

OBJECT X-RAYS

What can X-rays tell us about man-made objects?

Most modern electronic devices can be used without needing to look at the technology inside. In fact, opening up these objects often risks breaking all the delicate parts. So studying an X-ray picture is one way to satisfy your curiosity. X-ray images of electronic objects often look like maps — the wires are like roads, crossing over each other and carrying power to all the working parts. You may also be able to spot the circuit boards. These have paths printed on them for the power to follow, which means that fewer tangled wires are needed!

Have man-made objects changed over the years?

Yes — one hundred years ago the mechanical inventions of the day were fairly straightforward. They were designed so that they could be examined and repaired by lifting up a flap or taking off a panel. Back then the damaged parts were larger and easier to spot.

X-CEPTIONAL TECHNOLOGY

This picture of a **laptop computer** is made up of an X-ray photograph and a normal photograph, so that you can see the keys. The first portable computer was invented in 1981 and had a screen only five inches across.

The first printed **circuit board** was made in 1936 by the Austrian inventor **Paul Eisler**.

Barbara Blackburn is the world's **fastest typist** — she can type **212 words** a minute.

Time to play! Game consoles are really home computers designed to play games. The first home game console was the Magnavox Odyssey. Released in 1972, it was powered by batteries and had no sound, but came with 12 games.

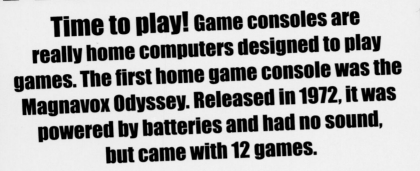

INSIDE A CONSOLE ARE CIRCUIT BOARDS, MEMORY UNITS, AND A BLU-RAY OR DVD PLAYER. IF YOU LOOK CAREFULLY, YOU CAN SEE WHERE THE DVD GOES.

►TODAY, CONTROLLERS ARE OFTEN WIRELESS — THEY DON'T NEED TO BE ATTACHED TO THE CONSOLE TO WORK.

Can you guess what the large black circle inside this cell phone is? It's a **speaker**. Also inside is a circuit board, a microphone, and an LCD screen ("LCD" stands for "liquid crystal display").

Ring ring! The first **cell phone call** was made in **1973**.

Many cell phones are equipped with **GPS** and can be tracked by **satellite** all over the world.

Tune in . . . This **X-ray** shows an **MP3 player** with its own set of earphones. **MP3 players** can carry thousands of songs, and even videos, inside their **memory chips.**

Here you can see the **earphone jack** slotting neatly into the MP3 player's **socket.**

Very few X-rays are absorbed by this **screen**, giving a clear view of the **circuit boards** beneath.

MP3 players can be attached to speakers to share your songs with your friends. This is called a docking station.

SPEAKERS TURN THE ELECTRONIC SIGNALS FROM THE MP3 PLAYER INTO SOUND VIBRATIONS.

The **speaker** diaphragm, or **cone**, is made from compressed **paper**.

Circuit boards take the **electronic signals** from the MP3 player and send them to the **speakers.**

Wires attached to the edge of the speaker make the diaphragm **vibrate.**

SOUND VIBRATIONS MAKE YOUR EARDRUMS VIBRATE, TOO — AND THIS IS HOW WE HEAR SOUNDS.

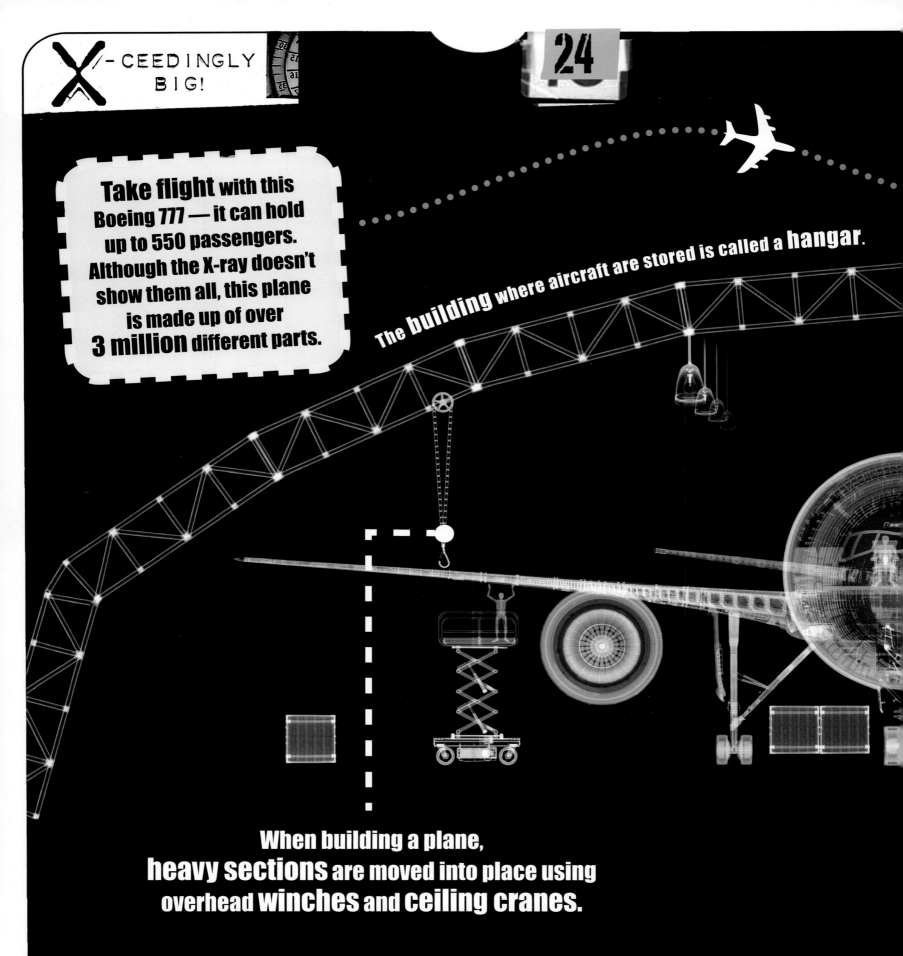

Take flight with this Boeing 777 — it can hold up to 550 passengers. Although the X-ray doesn't show them all, this plane is made up of over **3 million** different parts.

The **building** where aircraft are stored is called a **hangar**.

When building a plane, **heavy sections** are moved into place using overhead **winches** and **ceiling cranes**.

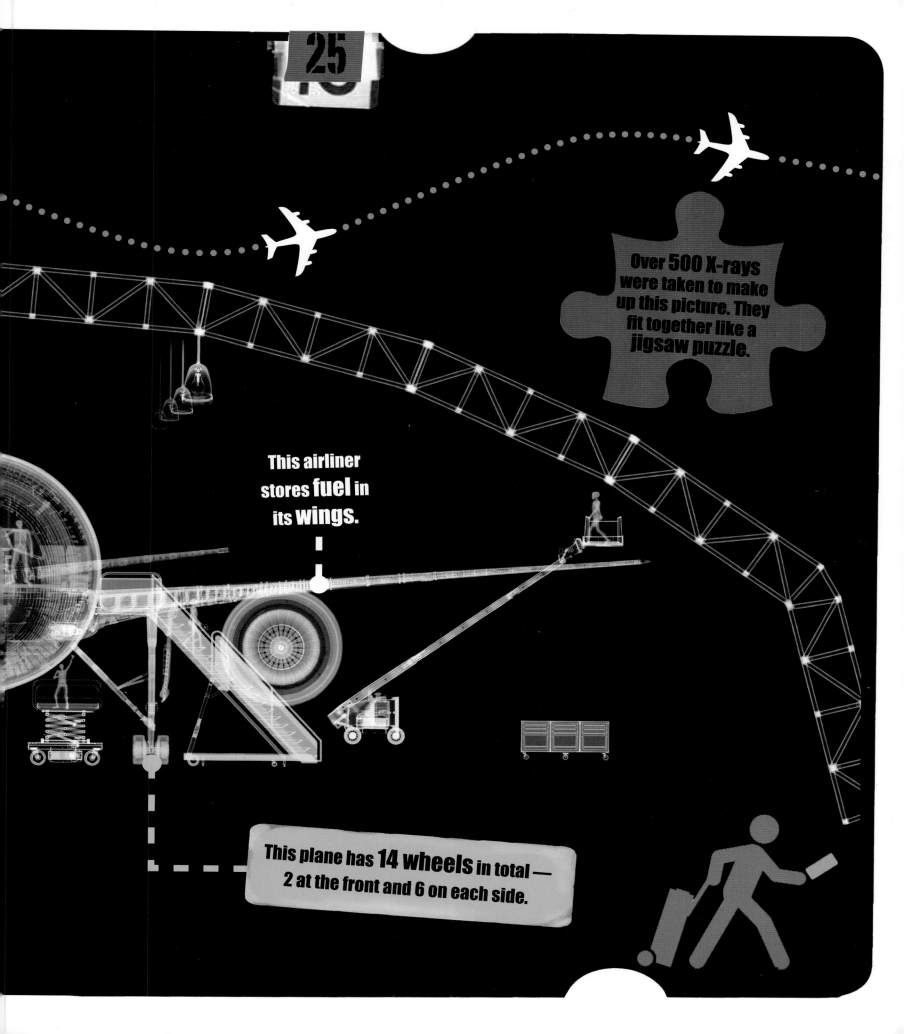

Over 500 X-rays were taken to make up this picture. They fit together like a jigsaw puzzle.

This airliner stores **fuel** in its **wings**.

This plane has **14 wheels** in total — 2 at the front and 6 on each side.

NATURE X-RAYS

What can X-rays tell us about nature?
In the next few pages we'll look at bats, insects, and other creatures to find out some of nature's greatest secrets. The exact way in which bats are able to fly suddenly becomes clear in an X-ray photograph. And the number of chambers in a nautilus shell could otherwise only be guessed from the outside.

Are X-rays of animals similar to X-rays of humans?
Yes — X-rays of animals have the same advantages. They allow us to see what's going on inside the animal without having to cut it open. This is useful for vets when they are trying to cure sick animals. It is also helpful to scientists who study animals in order to understand how they work.

Look at the **jointed legs** of this **Chilean rose hair tarantula.** If this spider ever loses a leg, it can grow a new one in its place.

Spiders are not insects — they are members of the **arachnid** class.

Although a tarantula has fearsome fangs and a venomous bite, it is not considered to be lethal to healthy humans.

Can you see the backbone running down the center of this **red snapper**? A flexible backbone allows the fish to bend its body to swim through the water.

FISH do not need to breathe oxygen from the **AIR**.

They use the **OXYGEN** already dissolved in the **WATER**.

Fish have been on Earth for **500 million years**. There are about **30,000** different **species** alive today.

A fish takes in **dissolved oxygen** through its **gills**.

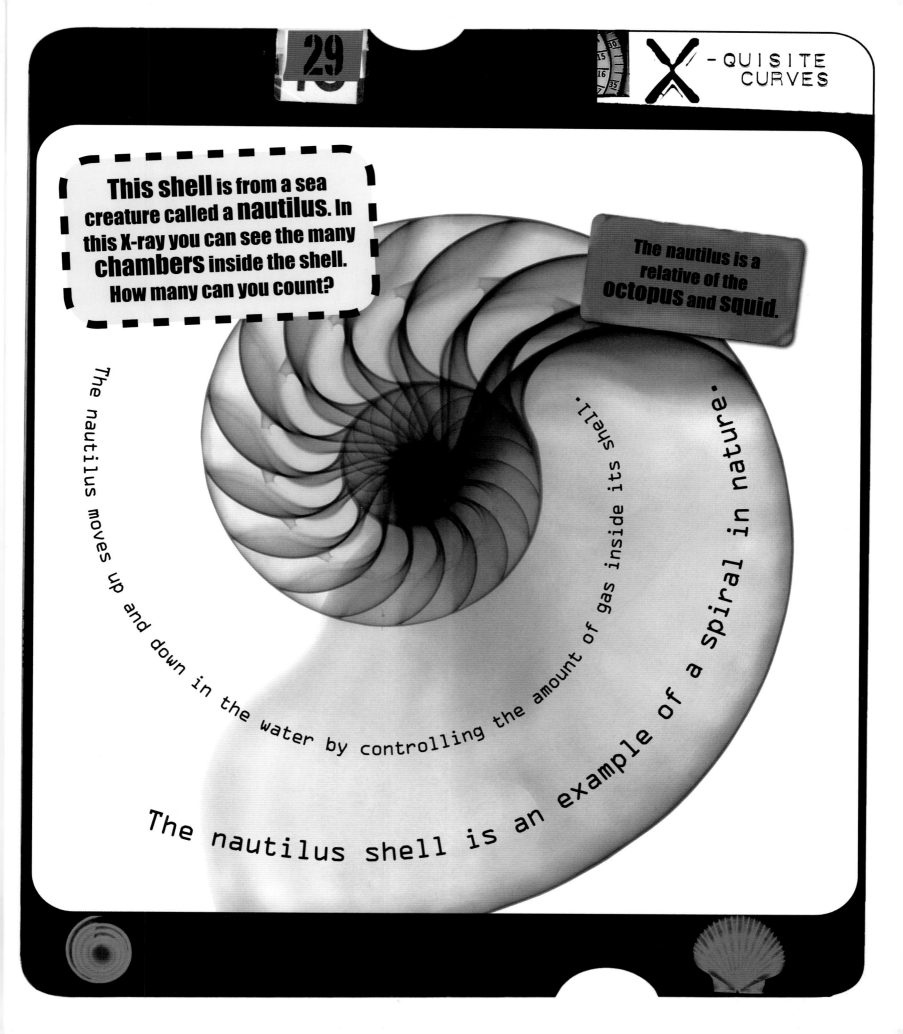

This shell is from a sea creature called a **nautilus**. In this X-ray you can see the many **chambers** inside the shell. How many can you count?

The nautilus is a relative of the **OCTOPUS** and **squid**.

The nautilus moves up and down in the water by controlling the amount of gas inside its shell.

The nautilus shell is an example of a spiral in nature.

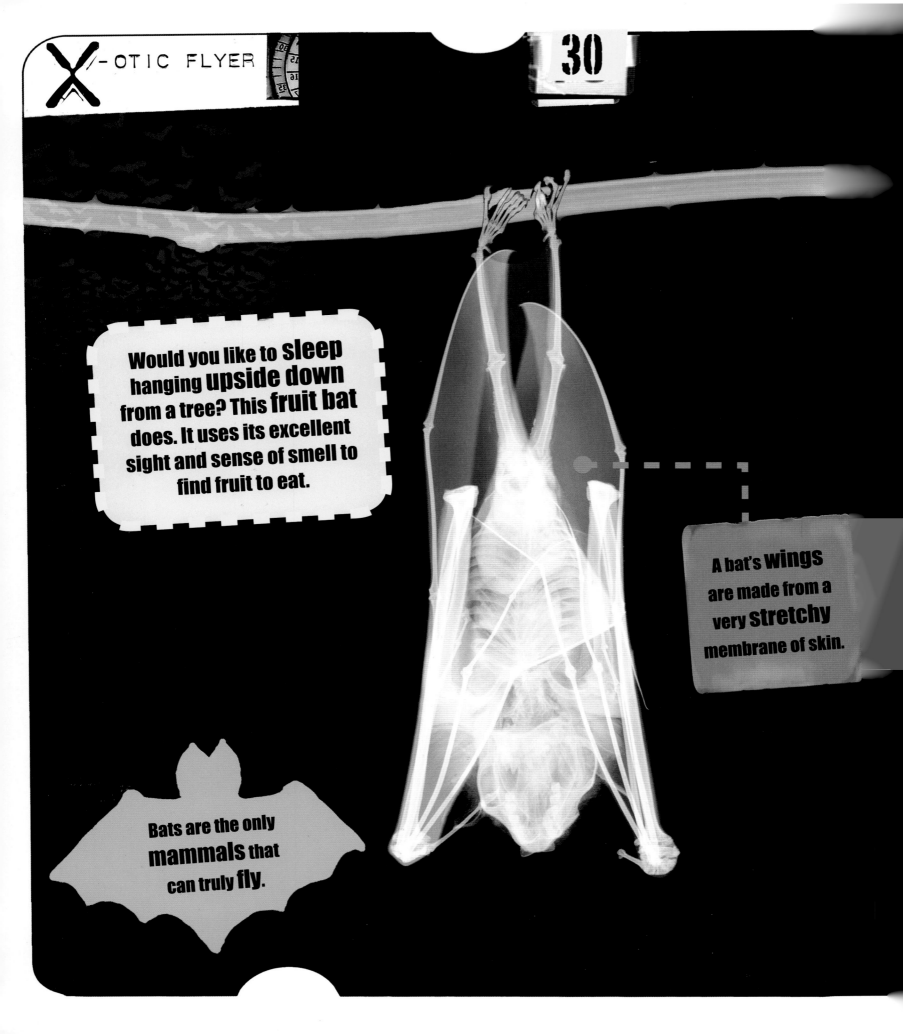

The bones in a bat's wings are actually long finger bones.

Most bats find their way using sonar. They shout out, then wait to hear the echo of the sound bouncing back to them. This helps them to judge their distance from other objects.

Fruit bats have a wingspan measuring up to six feet.

Count the wings on this longhorn beetle . . . It has two pairs, but uses only the lower set for flight. At up to six inches in length, it is one of the biggest beetles in the world.

The beetle's **fearsome jaws** are called **mandibles**.

Male beetles use their **antennae** to detect females. It is these **"long horns"** that give this family of beetles its name.

The scarab beetle was thought by the ancient Egyptians to symbolize a sun god called Khepri. Like all other insects, beetles have **six legs**.

An **INSECT'S** tough outer shell is called its **EXOSKELETON**.

Can you see any bones? No — the insect's hard shell does the job instead!

Look at the **claws** on this crab! One of them is huge and can be used for crushing. The largest species of crab is the Japanese spider crab — a relative of this one.

Why do you think this strong, tough **claw** looks **white?** It's because it absorbs lots of **X-rays.**

If a **JAPANESE SPIDER CRAB** stretched out its **CLAWS**, the distance would be as long as **TWO TALL MEN** lying head to toe.

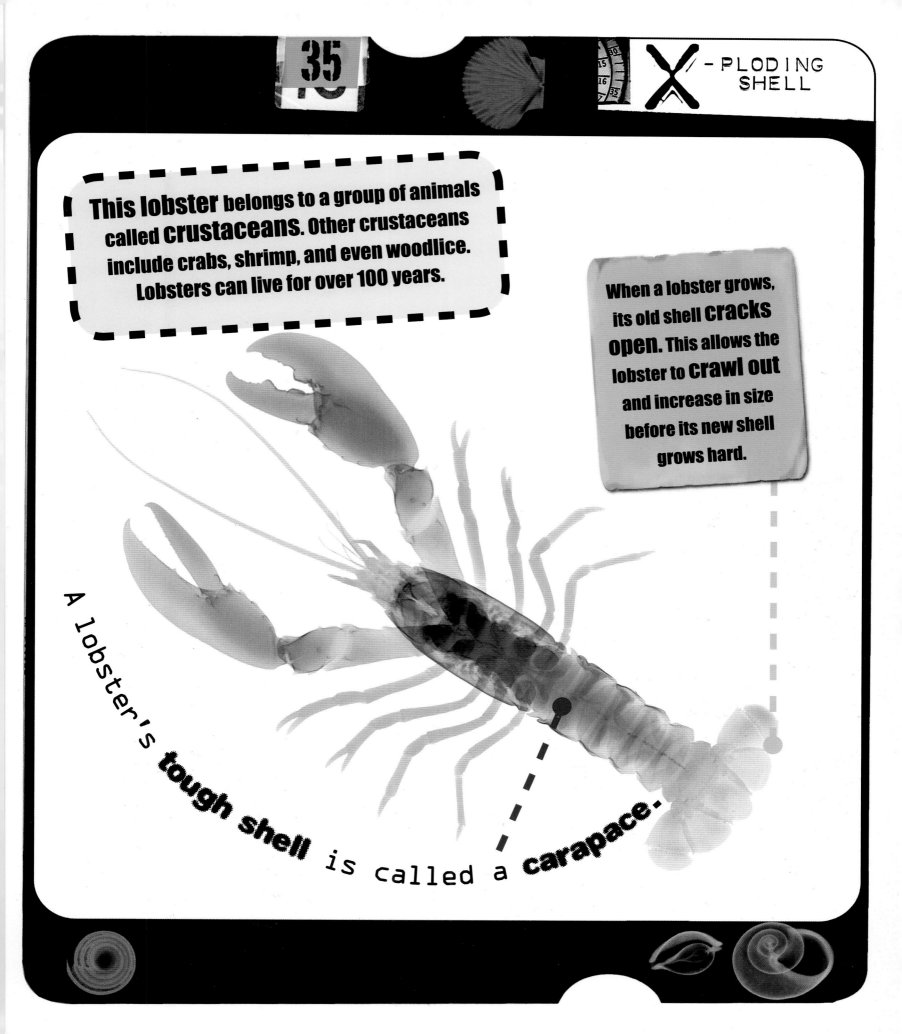

This lobster belongs to a group of animals called **crustaceans**. Other crustaceans include crabs, shrimp, and even woodlice. Lobsters can live for over 100 years.

When a lobster grows, its old shell **cracks open**. This allows the lobster to **crawl out** and increase in size before its new shell grows hard.

A lobster's **tough shell** is called a **carapace**.

SPORTS X-RAYS

NEARLY THERE!

Why are X-rays important to sports players?
People who play competitive sports at the highest level need a lot of looking after. All those hours of training and competing can take a toll on the body, leaving it at risk of injury. Using X-rays to find out what might be wrong is a very useful way of keeping healthy.

Are some sports more dangerous than others?
Yes. If the athlete is playing a contact sport, such as football or rugby, then the chances of getting injured are much higher. Bashing into other players is always likely to result in some kind of injury.

What else can sports X-rays show us?
They reveal the secrets of an athlete's equipment, too. We can view how shoulder pads fit on a football player, or which parts of a helmet are the strongest. As you will see, there's more to an athlete than just his or her body.

This tennis player's spine twists and curves as his body moves and rotates. Can you see the spare tennis ball in the pocket of the player's shorts?

Why do you think this tennis ball looks **black?** It's because it's full of **air**.

There are **26 bones** in the **human foot.**

Athletes use different styles of running for different lengths of races. Sprinters run on the balls of their feet. Long-distance athletes use their heels and toes as they run.

toes

ball

heel

The BONE at the base of the spine is the remains of the TAIL our ancient ancestors had.

The **Weight** of the human head and our upright stance actually make **balancing** very tricky.

The **fastest human** can run at a maximum speed of up to 30 miles per hour. **Cheetahs** are the fastest land animals and can travel at over 60 miles per hour.

Can you **believe** it? When you run, **both feet** are in the air at the **same time**!

The top layer of a **running track** is made of **rubber.**

This race car driver wears fireproof clothing in case of accidents. He also uses a protective helmet made from carbon fiber and plastic foam, materials that keep it light but strong.

The world's fastest car is called the **Thrust SSC**. Its record-breaking speed is a colossal **763 miles per hour.**

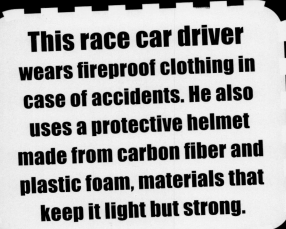

Broken legs are a common injury for race car drivers.

What a catch! This baseball glove fits on the right hand, which means that it belongs to a left-handed player. Players didn't wear gloves until the 1870s.

Baseballs are made from two pieces of white leather **stitched** together.

The first recorded game of **baseball** was played in **1846.**

Hup hup hup! These players are standing in the center's position, ready to pass the ball back at the start of a play. All football players wear protective padding on their bodies, especially the shoulders, thighs, and knees.

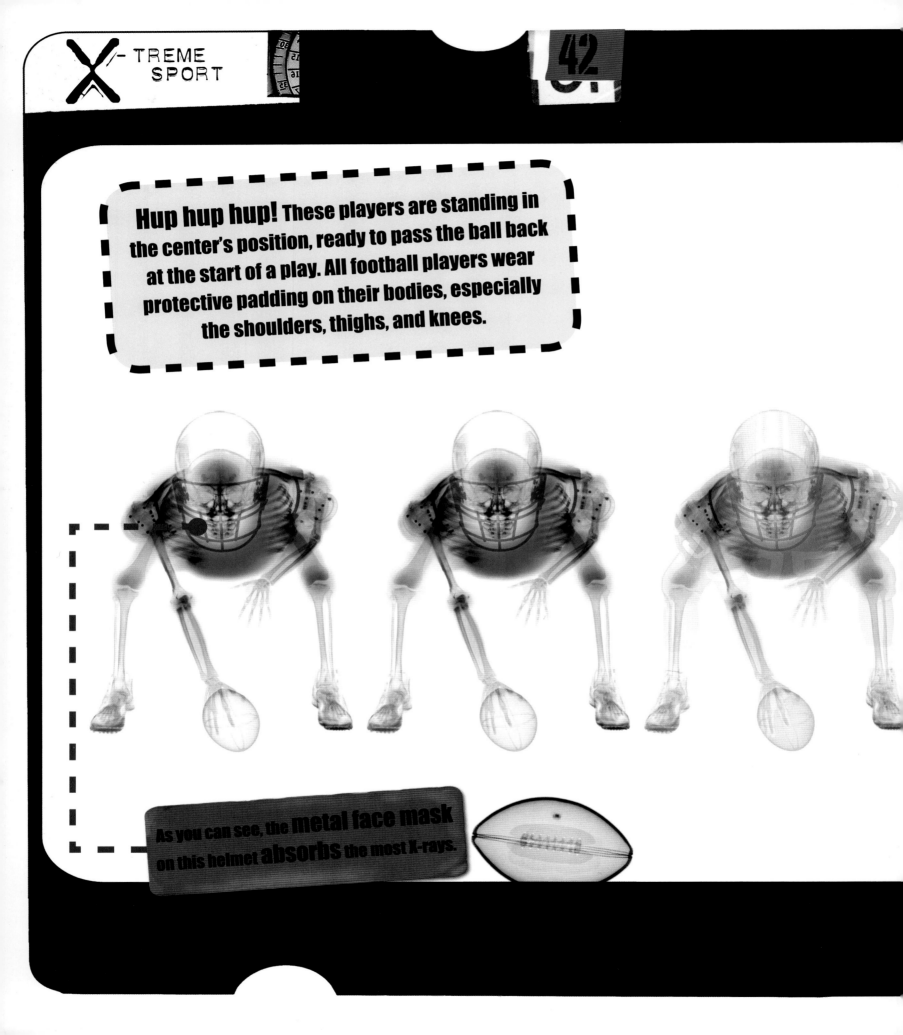

As you can see, the **metal face mask** on this helmet **absorbs** the most X-rays.

An **X-ray** photograph has been combined with a **normal** photograph to create this image. It shows us how the football player's **skeleton** provides the **structure** for his body.

Helmets protect players from serious **head injury.**

Football teams can contain up to **80 players.**

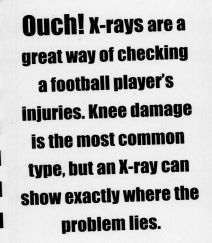

Ouch! X-rays are a great way of checking a football player's injuries. Knee damage is the most common type, but an X-ray can show exactly where the problem lies.

Sometimes a player's **shoulder** pops out of its **socket** — this is called a dislocated shoulder and is a common injury.

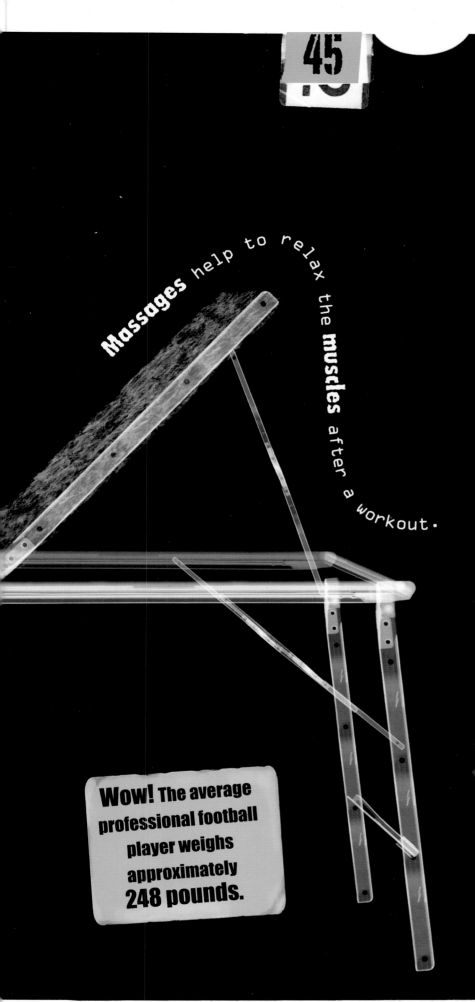

Massages help to relax the **muscles** after a workout.

Many injuries are thought to be the result of playing on **artificial fields**, which are **very hard.**

American football is such a **tough sport** that the average career lasts only **3.5 years.**

Wow! The average professional football player weighs approximately **248 pounds.**

BE AN X-RAY X-PERT!

Doctors, scientists, and other experts need to know what to look for when examining an X-ray photograph. It's all about having a good eye for detail and an ability to recognize the different parts that make up a person, animal, or thing.

Here's your chance to test your own skills and become an X-ray X-pert! Take a look at these X-ray details, and then go back through the book to see if you can find which photograph each one belongs to. **Good luck!**

A
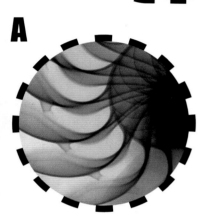

B
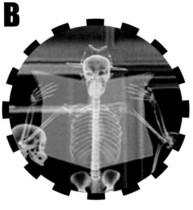

C

D
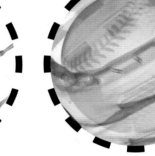

E
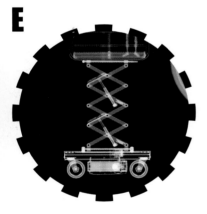

F
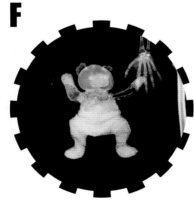

G
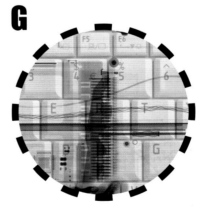

H

I
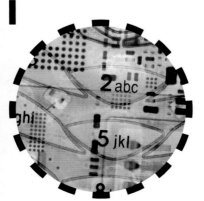

J

K

L
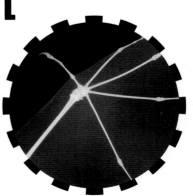

M

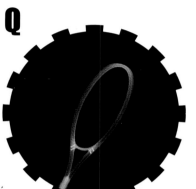

N

O

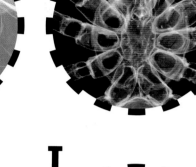

P

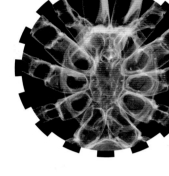

Q

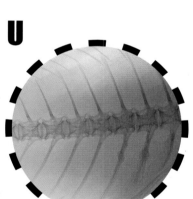

R

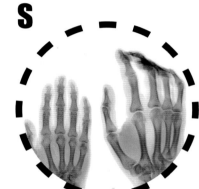

S

T

U

V

W

X

Y

Z